MathStart®
CAPACITY

by Stuart J. Murphy • illustrated by Sylvie Wickstrom

HarperCollinsPublishers

LEVEL
3

ROOM for RIPLEY

To Dixie and a ripple-free recovery
—S.J.M.

To Thor
—S.W.

HarperCollins®, ☙®, and MathStart® are registered trademarks of HarperCollins Publishers.
For more information about the MathStart series, write to HarperCollins Children's Books,
10 East 53rd Street, New York, NY 10022.

Bugs incorporated in the MathStart series design were painted by Jon Buller.

ROOM FOR RIPLEY
Text copyright © 1999 by Stuart J. Murphy
Illustrations copyright © 1999 by Sylvie Wickstrom
Manufactured in China. All rights reserved.
Visit our web site at http://www.harperchildrens.com

Library of Congress Cataloging-in-Publication Data
Murphy, Stuart J., date
    Room for Ripley / by Stuart J. Murphy ; illustrated by Sylvie Wickstrom.
        p.   cm. — (MathStart)
    "Capacity, level 3."
    Summary: Uses a story about a young boy who is getting a fish bowl ready for his new
pet to introduce various units of liquid measure.
    ISBN 0-06-027620-7. — ISBN 0-06-027621-5 (lib. bdg.). — ISBN 0-06-446724-4 (pbk.)
    1. Volume (Cubic content)—Juvenile literature.   [1. Volume (Cubic content)   2. Liquids—
Measurement.]   I. Wickstrom, Sylvie, ill.
II. Title.   III. Series.
QA465.M86   1999   98-26109
530.8—dc21   CIP
                                                                                                                          AC

Typography by Elynn Cohen
10
❖
First Edition

Carlos visited the fish at Mr. Peterson's pet store every day. The quick little guppy was his favorite. He made so many ripples when he flashed through the water that Carlos called him Ripley. He would watch Ripley until Ana, his sister, said they had to leave.

Carlos wanted to buy Ripley with his
allowance. "First you'll need to make a
good home for your fish," said Ana.

She found her old fish bowl in the attic. "I used to have fish myself. I can teach you all about them," she said. "Put some water in the bowl and let it sit for a while. The water needs to be room temperature."

Carlos ran to the kitchen, got a measuring cup, and filled it with water. Then he poured it into the bowl. He knew he would need lots more.

1 CUP

9

Carlos emptied another
cup of water into the bowl.
Now it held a pint of water.

He tried to picture Ripley
swimming around. A pint
didn't look like nearly enough.

10

2 CUPS

equal

1 PINT

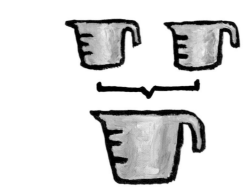

Ana found a bag of gravel, some seashells, and a little blue castle. Carlos dumped some gravel into the bowl. Then he carefully placed the castle in the gravel.

"The water doesn't even reach the top of the castle," said Ana.

"Don't worry, I'm going to add some more," said Carlos.

Carlos added two more cups—another pint. Now there was a quart of water in the bowl. "That's double the water we had before. Now the whole castle is underwater," said Carlos.

4 CUPS

equal

2 PINTS

equal

1 QUART

The next day Carlos and Ana stopped at the pet store and watched Ripley play tag with another fish. "Let's call the other one Wiggles," said Ana as the two fish darted around the tank.

"I need some plants for my fishbowl, Mr. Peterson," said Carlos. "Tomorrow I'm coming back to buy Ripley."

When the plants were in place, Carlos stepped back to look at Ripley's new home. "It still doesn't look like there's enough water, especially compared to the tank at the store," he thought.

Carlos added four more cups. That made another quart of water. Now there was a half gallon of water in the bowl.

8 CUPS

equal

4 PINTS

equal

2 QUARTS

equal

1 HALF GALLON

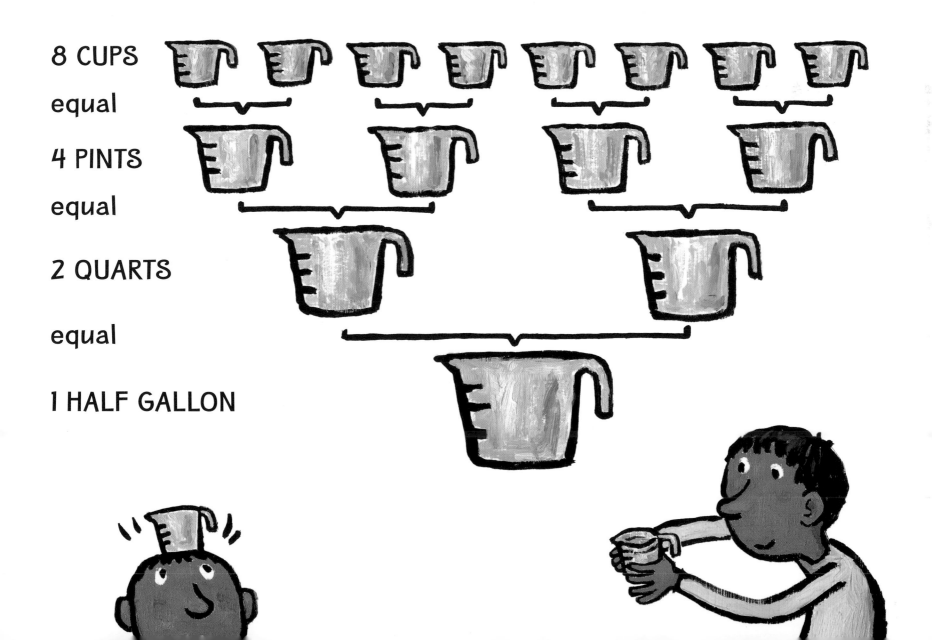

Carlos wondered what it would feel like to swim through the castle.

"I hope Ripley won't miss Wiggles when he comes home," said Carlos.

"I think he'll be happy as long as he has plenty of water and you take good care of him," said Ana.

Just to be sure, Carlos put eight cups of water into a pail. Then he emptied the pail into the bowl. Now the bowl had a full gallon of water.

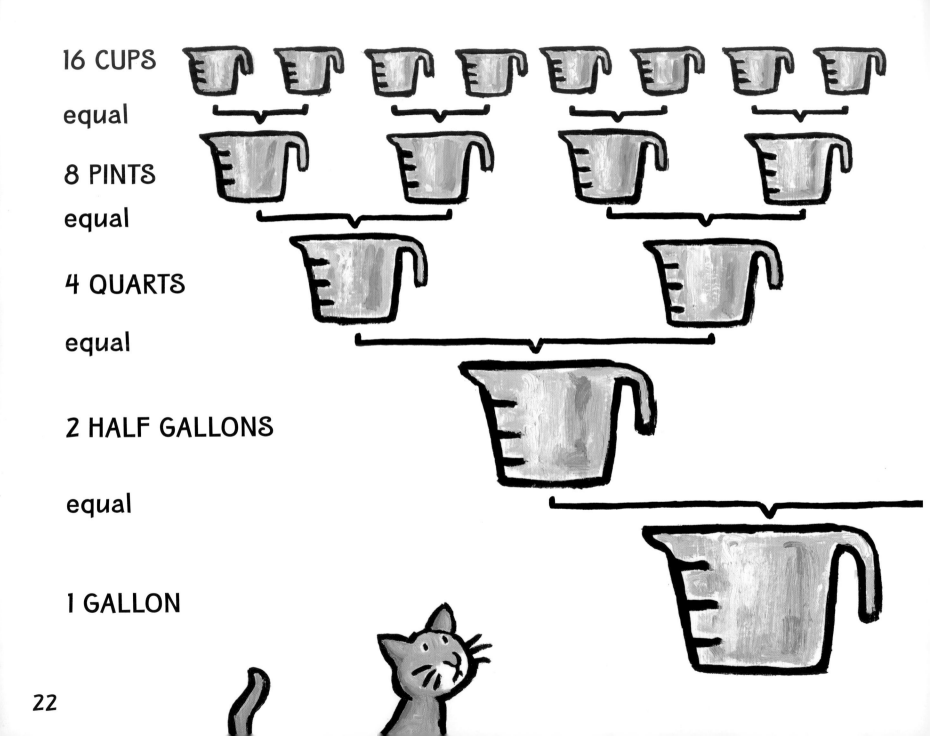

16 CUPS

equal

8 PINTS

equal

4 QUARTS

equal

2 HALF GALLONS

equal

1 GALLON

22

"I think there's room for Ripley now," said Ana as she attached her old filter. "And by tomorrow, the water will be just the right temperature for him."

That night Carlos could
hardly sleep. After school he
and Ana ran all the way to
the pet store.

Guppies
$1.29
each

Carlos gave his money to Mr. Peterson, who put Ripley into a little plastic bag filled with water. "So long, Ripley," said Mr. Peterson.

Wiggles looked a little lonely swimming around the tank without Ripley.

At home Ana told Carlos, "We'll need to let Ripley get used to his new home." First they floated the bag in the fish bowl. Then they emptied the bag—water, Ripley, and all—into the bowl.

Ripley moved around slowly. He swam around his
castle. He glided through his plants. He hardly made
any ripples at all.

"He looks kind of sad," said Carlos. "I bet he misses
his friend Wiggles."

"Surprise!" Ana shouted as she took a small plastic bag from behind her back. "You added so much water that there's not only room for Ripley, there's room for Wiggles, too!"

Soon Ripley and Wiggles were swimming around
and playing tag again—just as happy as could be.

In *Room for Ripley*, the math concept is measuring capacity using cups, pints, quarts, half gallons, and gallons.

If you would like to have more fun with the math concepts presented in *Room for Ripley*, here are a few suggestions:

• Read the story with the child and talk about what is going on in each picture.

• Ask questions throughout the story, such as: "How much water is in the tank now?" "Do you think that will be enough for Ripley, or will Carlos have to add more?" "Is a pint more or less than a quart?"

• Give the child a measuring cup and a large jar or container. Have the child estimate how many cups of water it will take to fill the jar, and then keep track of the cups as he or she fills the container with water. After the container is filled, help the child figure out the capacity of the container. Is it approximately a pint? a quart? a half gallon? a gallon?

• Look in your kitchen or supermarket and identify items like milk, water, or cottage cheese that come in containers of different capacities. What comes in cups? in pints? in quarts? in half gallons? in gallons?

You can do some of these activities and the ones on the following page with metric measures as well. For example, you can search for liter containers in your kitchen or supermarket, or find three containers that have the same capacity as a liter container.

Following are some activities that will help you extend the concepts presented in *Room for Ripley* into a child's life.

Cooking: Make a simple recipe such as instant pudding. Figure out how much more of each ingredient you would need if you wanted to double the recipe.

Party: When your child has friends over, ask what they would like to drink. Have the child figure out how much juice or soda you need if everyone gets one cup of his or her favorite drink. What if everyone wants two cups?

Around the House: Have the child fill a half-gallon container with water. Then help him or her find three other containers that he or she thinks will hold the same amount of water. Pour the water from the half-gallon container into the other containers to see if they do have the same capacity.

The following books include similar concepts to those that are presented in *Room for Ripley:*

- A CAKE ALL FOR ME by Karen Magnuson Beil

- PRETEND SOUP AND OTHER REAL RECIPES: *A Cookbook for Preschoolers & Up* by Mollie Katzen and Ann Henderson

- MEASURING UP! *Experiments, Puzzles, and Games Exploring Measurement* by Sandra Markle